"Flute". Ken 'Scotty' Lawrence.

AFTER POEMS, PSALMS

ALSO BY JOHN ROBERT LEE

St Lucian (1988)
Artefacts (2000)
Canticles (2007)
Elemental (2008)
Sighting (2013)
City Remembrances (2016)
Song and Symphony (2016)
Collected Poems 1975-2015 (2017)
Pierrot (2020)
Belmont Portfolio (2023)
Ikons (2023)

JOHN ROBERT LEE

AFTER POEMS, PSALMS

GLOSAS

PEEPAL TREE

First published in Great Britain in 2025
Peepal Tree Press Ltd
17 King's Avenue
Leeds LS6 1QS
UK

ISBN 13: 9781845236007

ACKNOWLEDGEMENTS

Some of these poems have been published in Acalabash.com.

Thanks to:
Cover Art: *Poems from Saint Lucia* by Sir Llewellyn Xavier, Saint Lucia.

The artist writes: *Poems from Saint Lucia* is a series of visual songs. An arrangement of colours and an attempt to understand the complexity of form. The focus shifts from colour to texture to form and blurs the boundaries between painting and sculpture. *Poems from Saint Lucia* envisages an island with clean rivers, where mermaids bathe in pools of crystal clear water. Where the roads are lined with flowering trees full of fruit, where communication cables are buried beneath the shadowy streets, where the population benefits from a constant supply of fresh, clean water. A plastic-free country, where disputes are settled peacefully. An island where art and culture are celebrated and the greatness of Saint Lucia's poets, writers, musicians and artists is honoured. Where mercy and truth embrace each other in a symphony of love.

Frontispiece: "Flute" by Ken 'Scotty' Lawrence, Saint Lucia. After photo by Frank Norville.

Author photo: Veronica Lee

For brief quotations from the work of Wendell Berry, Philip Sherrard, Saint Lucian folk singers.

Jeremy Poynting and Peepal Tree Press.

CONTENTS

For

The Psalmist

Writers and artists of faith in the sacred and sacramental

In Memoriam

Edward Baugh, Jamaican scholar and poet, 1936 - 2023
Funso Aiyejina, Nigerian/Trinidadian poet and scholar, 1949 – 2024
Irvin Desir, Saint Lucian poet, 1954 - 2024
Velma Pollard, Jamaican writer and scholar, 1937 - 2025
Hazel Simmons-McDonald, St Lucian scholar and writer, 1947-2025

After poems, psalms. And canticles of island pilgrims
passing through self-important harbours, smoke-blue banana valleys,
villages lounging at the curves of bougainvillea lanes." – J. R. Lee
(Canticles)

"*. . . without participation in God, there can be no escaping fragmentation, disintegration, self-alienation, however much we may struggle against them. . . . .only when his art possesses a sacred quality will it present a positive challenge to our technological world and to the degradation of human life which is endemic to it. . . the task of the artist – of the sacred artist – is to reveal to us and to itself, the true nature of a world that we have allowed ourselves to regard as non-sacred, non-sacramental, merely neutral, if not simply dead or soulless matter;"*
– Philip Sherrard (The Sacred in Life and Art).

". . . The world
is a holy vision, had we clarity
to see it – a clarity that men
depend on men to make."
– Wendell Berry (Collected Poems)

I – PROLOGUE

Now also when I am old and greyheaded,
O God do not forsake me,
Until I declare Your strength to this generation,
Your power to everyone who is to come. – *Psalm 71:18*

1.
Inexorably, irrevocably, I draw near the High Place –
bamboo-fluting of wood doves,
coconut palms shuttling the breeze,

Morne Gimie wreathed with overcast evening,
woodsmoke dissolving its plumes over Garrand,
anonymous traffic of voices, music, cars outside on the road,

and news of another passing lingers
with intermittent drizzle,
end-of-day gospelling blackbirds –

Now also when I am old and greyheaded,

2.
still wanting that blood-warmth of affectionate arms,
those soft eyes of caring desire,
lovingkind words which affirm

yes, certainties of covenant secure
against streetsmart chatter of infidelities,
mundane idolatries,

insidious seductions of cyberspace we finger
to distraction, shutting our hearts away
in virtual isolation with selfies –

O God do not forsake me,

3.
when names dodge familiar faces,
anxieties trouble sleep and speech, when
we collapse in once firm and potent places,

when dollars never meet estimated ends,
and LORD, when newly-fashioned plantocrats
turn these hapless island-nations to big-boat destinations,

and the people jam streets with pagan noise,
vote their birthrights to corrupt parliaments –
LORD, extend Your mercy to the young ones

Until I declare Your strength to this generation,

4.

with my horn of words that sound true,
muted with love from blasted blaring,
scaling the beauty of the blue

and other notes, measuring solo lines
with faith, bridging our earth
to Your great and Holy Kingdom,

weaving chords of canticles to birth
light again, counterpoint dark again,
to raise Your praise, to unveil again Your High Home,

Your power to everyone who is to come.

II

He shall be like a tree
Planted by the rivers of water,
That brings forth its fruit in its season,
Whose leaf also shall not wither; – Psalm 1: 3

1.
Try for another angle in the confessional,
a different look at the private, the collective,
of days darting like birds' shadows

at eyes' corners, under slowing reflexes,
over the impossible obituaries,
aspiring autocrats and their absurdities –

you don't want to repeat yourself,
to sketch worn images again,
to wallow in self-righteous pity, forgetting

He shall be like a tree

2.
not a pigeon-encrusted monument
to be pulled down from its base of lies,
not other related shifty-eyed impotencies –

so you must enter the aloneness
of honesties, consort with shifting fictions
of memory, desire again ghosts that haunt

passages of your flesh and sly mind,
find, if you can, where you lost, or found, your way,
to know who caught you up with quiet laughter, and

Planted by the rivers of water,

3.
hiding baffled tears under cold gazes,
still too innocent, naïve about circling motives,
raise what you know, the truth of things in this galaxy,

parables seated at the heart of myths,
fantasy chronicles, prophecies,
tales of broken cities –

but note they have other interests,
titillating distractions, the mind
with whom you may try to reason,

That brings forth its fruit in its season,

4.

sooner or later, one way or the other;
so, look again, see again,
to glimpse an epiphany,

to hold quickly an insight,
to grasp some mystery of us
which was something of a bother

or a nameless fear,
or a persistent desire for something more
in the closer future, for us

Whose leaf also shall not wither.

III

Why do the nations rage,
And the people plot a vain thing?
The kings of the earth set themselves,
And the rulers take counsel together, – Psalm 2: 1,2

1.
The BBC man intoned with Big Ben tolling,
"that metronome of grief", queues
circled in rectangular vigils

about the rosemary, myrtle and oak wreath,
family shifted under the gossiping gazing
of the world gathering

across streets and screens
to see the back of the retreating piper
shutting this Elizabethan age –

Why do the nations rage,

2.
commonwealth of the once enslaved,
the massacred, boot-trampled colonies
of this empire enriched

by pirates, arrogant armies, hanging governors,
fat bishops? Make reparation they say to the barons,
apologise, they write to the king,

to our royalty and citizens below the Atlantic –
our children without memory
want rest; how long will Europe and their kind hate our skin

And the people plot a vain thing?

3.
They made the White Man a counterfeit Christ,
Whiteness their religion and manifesto,
spread the mind-destroying disease of Colonialism,

plundered God's rich earth and its coloured peoples
under the red, white and blue of that unholy triad –
But the King with hair like wool, Himself,

the One on the rainbow throne, Just and Holy,
the Anointed, whose promises are certain,
who sees all things, against whose Majesty

The kings of the earth set themselves,

4.

He knows His own, the oppressed of the earth,
and He will deliver in His appointed time –
even now, the wand is broken,

crown removed, orb and scepter laid down
at the feet of the Most High (let him who have eyes, see),
the commonwealth starting to scatter –

let the people of Jah go out of Babylon,
flee Sodom and Gomorrah, abandon Egypt,
let revelations be opened again by the prophets,

And the rulers take counsel together.

IV

But You, O LORD, are a shield for me,
My glory and the One who lifts up my head.
I cried to the Lord with my voice,
And He heard me from His holy hill. Selah. – Psalm 3: 3, 4

1.
We live here, however the life is,
in cavernous cities, on sinking islands,
famine-infested deserts, flooding plateaus,

with mass shootings, insurrections, invasions,
hysteria of right-wing media harassing
blacks, women and the liberal democracy

that allows muslims, atheists and pride caravans
to parade their choice down main street,
while stoning girls and slaughtering journalists mark medieval
theocracies –

But You, O LORD, are a shield for me,

2.
when armed gangs rule these kanaval and konpa destinations,
when sidewalks are tainted with blood,
highways littered with broken metal and dead bodies

from speeding maniacs; when dance hall stars
ride riddims to shoot informers,
and push explicit lyrics of hard-core porn;

and when autocrats despise laws,
squander the little we have,
deny the people's ballot choices, you Dread, are

My glory and the One who lifts up my head.

3.
And when in the flesh of my love,
under grapefruit and avocado blossoms,
gazing at the rose of sharon turning pink

below the overcast sky, when in my love
I hunger for more than is possible
in this aging, baffled body with its searching face,

probing answers I had with doubts nagging
about now, then and tomorrow if it comes,
and we must go from each other to the promised House,

I cried to the Lord with my voice,

4.

I spoke aloud in kitchen and garden
from my knees, when no one was near,
no one visible, no one to comfort

and assure and say again that I was loved,
that I was cared for, that I should rise
and come pick some mangoes or guavas,

or walk together near the pumpkin and pineapples
with pup cavorting around our heels –
I spoke aloud with wet eyes to myself,

And He heard me from His holy hill. Selah.

V

What is man that You are mindful of him,
And the son of man that You visit him?
For You have made him a little lower than the angels,
And You have crowned him with glory and honour. – Psalm 8: 4, 5

1.
The monotonous heavy sound of persistent rain,
polyrhythmic syncopation of edges dripping
on gutters, concrete and leaves,

and somewhere, land slips, roads run
like flooding rivers, a man
drowns with his cow behind his home,

thunder explodes under apocalyptic lightning,
dogs howl, and we are grateful
to be spared the wind this time –

What is man that You are mindful of him,

2.
that he is not blown off the face of earth
for his deep-heart cruelties to others,
like the mutilated boy Emmett Till, 1941-1955,

abducted, tortured and lynched
in Mississippi, falsely accused of flirtation
with a white man's white woman,

the crime on view in his open casket,
which I remember now under storm,
and wonder about my humankind

And the son of man that You visit him?

3.
The boy Till, numberless other men
and women of my race under burning
crosses, bent knees, strangling holds

of Atlantic caravels, haunt the hurucans
that howl from Africa, their names
in the drumming, insistent rain,

their laments in the blues of psalms
that symphonies of night insects raise again –
and we meditate under sheets on the theology of man,

For You have made him a little lower than the angels,

4.

and made a covenant of salt with him,
seated him in a high pavilion
of priests and kings and queens,

sent to him, Ancient of days, Your Son of Man,
Who he lynched and nailed like a Negro,
like Emmett Till, the boy from Illinois –

amazing grace indeed, sing Aretha
and the storefront churches,
that You have given this man ransom and redemption,

And You have crowned him with glory and honour.

VI

You shall keep them, O LORD,
You shall preserve them from this generation forever.
The wicked prowl on every side,
When vileness is exalted among the sons of men. – *Psalm 12: 7, 8*

1.
We call holy convocations for the feasts of months,
of flute and drums, flowers rose and blue,
armies of song and dance in costumed ranks

coming from village halls to cathedrals to city squares
among green mornes, by oceans' edges,
and chantwelles chant the ancient word

of our story, *Ti Kongo asou lanmè*;
we have not forgotten coffle and barracoon,
stinking ships, the sea's hump-cruel road –

You shall keep them, O LORD,

2.
exiles in Babylon town, new world citizens
of Amerikkka, shipwrecked islanders,
survivors of many middle passages

that *Ti Kongo ja navidjé;* singing blues, kaiso and solo,
dancing lakonmèt, weedova and the solitary koutoumba,
sending to the world out of every generation

from these small places, minds bringing light
to the civilized darkness, which you wonder
if they will ever learn, that under skin, we are brethren –

You shall preserve them from this generation forever

3.
from self-hating, race-baiting supremacists; You shall hold them,
rooted in their reservoir of resilience, trodding to drum,
chak-chak and vyélon, in madras and foulard,

lè Ti Kongo ka sélébwé lafèt flè, émansipasyon, *andépandans –*
we are who we are, imago Dei, children of the first peoples,
enslaved Africans and others who came to these islands

to make creole nations, *péyi kwéyòl,* something new
in the fractured, separated world,
an archipelago on parade.

The wicked prowl on every side,

4.

as they have always done,
seducing with dollars and resorts,
turning the heads of leaders from the peoples' faith

to idols of Babylon, gods of Mammon, golden calves,
and the people forget themselves –
Ti Kongo ka pléwé pou mò manman'y,

his younger friends' blood clots streets,
discord across devices corrupting their hearts,
and the ancient wisdom of the tabernacles is lost, not remembered,

When vileness is exalted among the sons of men.

VII

But I have trusted in your mercy;
My heart shall rejoice in your salvation.
I will sing to the LORD,
Because He has dealt bountifully with me. – *Psalm 13: 5,6*

1.
After poems, psalms. And sacred canticles
that hymn the Divine Presence
in which we dance gracious quadrille

to the scratchy vyélon, mandolin,
chak-chak and goat-skin drum,
women in the alluring mystery

of their wob dwiyèt, men careful
with their feet – poems so often forget
the Dancer of creation laughing in the brown mud of our genesis –

But I have trusted in Your mercy;

2.
and sought the sacramental of my days
in the archetypal scissor-tailed gull
circling above sibilant surf,

in casuarinas' needle-leaved curtsies
before the breeze of angels' wings off a hill,
in elegant spider lilies under my crotons,

in the trusting gaze of the chained pup,
within the perfect mastery of Your sun settling its stained-glass saints
and evening offerings on the horizon's altar –

My heart shall rejoice in your salvation

3.
with blues and laments like Billie Holiday's of strange fruit,
with Marley's reggae to get up, stand up to the wicked man,
with Shadow and Rudder waving the high mas,

Patrick St. Eloi, Emeline Michel, Floreta Marquis,
and clay-voiced multitudes choiring out of their psalter –
among dancers, players of instruments,

we make psalms of our living before Your throne,
all of it, permutations and combinations
of joy, heartache, aging and diurnal boredom –

I will sing to the LORD,

4.

yesterday, today and tomorrow,
in lines and images from Your overwhelming creation,
in mantras and riddims from globes, maps, clocks of earth and
galaxies,

of the Simplicity of God,
of His Holy Sovereignty,
in Whose unity we are one diversity –

after poems, psalms. I raise chantings of faith
in the great I AM with cantors
of the tabernacles of the Holy Mystery,

Because He has dealt bountifully with me.

VIII

In my distress I called upon the LORD,
And cried out to my God;
He heard my voice from His temple,
And my cry came before Him, even to His ears. – Psalm 18: 6

1.
But how to render psalms into a profane world
that has desacralised the cosmos
with its liturgies of unbelief,

humanistic heresies,
desecration of every corner of earth,
blasphemous mockery of the Awe-full

Presence of God, its false premises of Reason –
a world that refuses reverence,
bowing down before itself as God.

In my distress, I called upon the LORD,

2.
I looked long into cryptograms
of fauna and flora, the imago Dei of children and kittens,
I did not dismiss intuitions and intimations

that come with trinities of butterflies, egrets and lilies,
and I listened to the Sons of Negus,
Count Ossie and Mystic Revelation, U Roy,

Carlene Davis, Ras Shorty I, Joseph Niles
and sincere choristers of our little churches,
waiting for the Spirit's direction,

And cried out to my God,

3.
so I might learn from these the tongue
of revelation, the word to translate
the mystical code in all creation,

the image and riddim, like a groundation drum,
that could entwine tight these here lines,
and bring someone, somewhere, to His Simplicity,

their imagination opening to the Holy,
to sacred reasoning and vision,
to *know* their place and themselves –

He heard my voice from His temple,

4.

and He gave me these ikons of a personal
and collective nature, my own ’itations
on the Sacredness of the Most High,

the Transcendent One; on the sacrilege of man,
his genocides and prejudices, his worship of Mammon,
and certain judgement by the Anointed Heir –

so we, disciples of the Logos, come to sanctuaries,
crypts, offices of scribes, the sacerdotal art,
and wait for coming of the first line, with helpless prayer –

And my cry came before Him, even to His ears.

IX

The law of the LORD is perfect, converting the soul;
The testimony of the LORD is sure, making wise the simple;
The statutes of the LORD are right, rejoicing the heart;
The commandment of the LORD is pure, enlightening the eyes; – Psalm 19:7,8.

1.
The sound-track of our chronicles
are the grammar, the syntax of nation languages,
chak-chak beat of old songs and their instruments,

kaiso and reggae, zouk and konpa,
afro-beat, dance-hall stylings of today –
how will the prophetic calling

of psalmists be heard beyond hard ears,
deep within minds floundering in pagan modernity,
unless past our white-washed history, we can sing

The law of the LORD is perfect, converting the soul

2.
with live coal of angels on our lips,
seeing the LORD high and lifted up,
seeing the degradation of the sacred cosmos,

our children bloodied in Babylon,
leaders playing power games on their platforms,
people easily bought with predictable promises –

in gardens of pigeon peas, avocado and breadfruit,
with fragrant marjoram and mint to distract,
we can despair in these island chapels, that

The testimony of the LORD is sure, making wise the simple.

3.
A side story of what relevance am not sure:
as a boy, every morning, with a lighted candle,
my father Alleyne had me read in his presence Psalm 35;

years later, with Rasta locks growing over my ears,
Ras Des encouraged me to "read the Psalms",
and I returned to the prayer book of the church and healing of
my hurts;

the Psalmist knows God and speaks directly to Him,
he knows himself and confesses his sins,
on enemies he calls down imprecations –

The statutes of the LORD are right, rejoicing the heart;

4.

so how to chant psalms as a modern-day minstrel,
a griot, into these dark ages, I ask again –
no formula available, no form prescribed,

bring your heart's clouding faith, broker of truth, your aging riddims,
into this no-truth, secular metaverse of idols
and graven on-line images of autocrats and superstars,

and know yourself planter, waterer, sower
of sacred cosmology, from some city of refuge,
and know the LORD alone, psalmist-poet, can give increase, because,

The commandment of the LORD is pure, enlightening the eyes;

X

Lift up your heads, O you gates! Lift up you everlasting doors!
And the King of glory shall come in.
Who is this King of glory?
The Lord of hosts, He is the King of glory. Selah. – Psalm 24;9,10.

1.
How quickly go days now, falling
around each others' incandescent evenings
of cricket choruses, dogs' nagging quarrels

at something, wind shouldering roughly
through mango groves,
cars backfiring past rows

of ficus hedges, voices coming and going under the night,
rain beginning its whip-lashing off trees and roof,
and my thoughts, Talitha, turn to Him at the end of these
    shortened days –

Lift up your heads, O you gates! Lift up you everlasting doors!

2.
the holy ones chant in processional
through their Book of Hours,
even against legions of mockers

who imagine there is no heaven,
no Word become Man to walk with us
at the sorry heart of our utter need,

no Creator who has abolished death
as he did for you Talitha, daughter of Jairus –
o that their tears would plunge like this hard, insistent rain,

And the King of glory shall come in

3.
with cleansing tongues of His Spirit's comforting fire,
with the light of truth that He is,
with the Father's incomprehensible merciful love –

this gospel is still washed and sealed in blood of martyrs,
its scriptures dismissed as fragments of myths, old wives' fables,
racist counterfeits of the Christ still used to deceive and control,

church and state in beds of compromise with beasts of Babylon –
but He has not left Himself without witness, those who have
    not genuflected
to Baal – and there come some who ask about this Healer,

Who is this King of glory?

4.

In our house of exile as in Egypt,
the captives ask what is His Name?
What is His Father's Name?

He is Immanuel, God with us, the Son of Man,
Lamb of the Passover atonement,
Conqueror of death and the lords of hell –

this, friend, is not religious hyperbole,
not cant or ranting, cultic, red-eyed fervour,
this is the scoffed-at revelation, that you will take or laugh away –

The Lord of hosts, He is the King of glory. Selah.

XI

Show me Your ways O LORD; Teach me Your paths.
Lead me in Your truth and teach me,
For You are the God of my salvation;
On You I wait all the day. – Psalm 25:4,5

1.
Is it possible that the barrage of noise and images
out of Babel, murderous quarrels,
conspiracy theories of deceivers and insurrectionists,

all local and distant breaking news,
are meant to keep our distracted eyes and memories
off that ninth hour on an old hill called Golgotha

in a still contested ancient city? Where a Man
whose Name is a curse to many, was nailed
to a cross on the Jewish Yom Kippur?

Show me Your ways O LORD; Teach me Your paths.

2.
Is it conceivable that proud, blasphemous man,
broadcasting the death of God, desecrating
the creation with unbelief and greed,

corrupting the imago Dei within him by his arrogance,
lost in brainy ignorance, worshipping himself,
was ransomed by the covenant of blood settled in Gethsemane?

And is it logical, can it be true, that in that ninth hour,
reconciliation was made for Adam's race
by the Passover Lamb on the altar of Calvary?

Lead me in Your truth and teach me,

3.
while perennial philosophies and religions
explain man's estrangement from God and himself
in various ways, even as scoffers dismiss

the sacred dimensions in which we live.
What explains our desires for peace, fellowship
and love? Why does man worship even idols of stone?

Biology, psychology, evolution may explain it for some,
but consider the ninth hour, its prologues and epilogues,
the Innocent One under such contempt, shame and humiliation –

For You are the God of my salvation;

4.

You were fixed to the turning point of human history,
scapegoat hammered to that holocaust of sacrifice in man's stead,
Your blood flowing behind the darkened veil of afternoon,

at that ninth hour, into the Most Holy Place.
We take the witness of faithful women at the tomb,
of martyrs who followed, and beyond betrayals

and denials, with searching, clouding faith,
we know something cosmic happened on that hill,
a new covenant was sealed in that bloodied Body. Lord Immanuel,

On You I wait all the day.

XII

The LORD is my light and my salvation;
Whom shall I fear?
The Lord is the strength of my life;
Of whom shall I be afraid? – Psalm 27:1

1.
And then the sacred vacancy
of linen cloths, garden tomb,
empty seat of the Stranger at the Emmaus inn,

bread and fish, glasses of wine,
guava cheese and tamarind balls
left as silent witnesses to the deserted conversation –

in Caravaggio's painting of the scene,
did the inn-keeper and his wife see anything odd?
Everything is changed by that Resurrection –

The LORD is my light and my salvation;

2.
the wand of death broken and abolished,
life unimaginably abundant beyond the sepulchre,
the Risen walks with us in the corridor of history, now,

the ancient kerygma proclamation announces
reconciliation with God and forgiven man
through the living, ascended Pantocrator,

the Serpent's head crushed by this Seed of Woman,
hell's captives freed by Elohim Incarnate,
whose return to us is promised in an approaching hour –

Whom shall I fear?

3.
His Resurrection changes everything –
coffins and cemeteries are not the last chapter,
dictators, assassins, lynch mobs,

hate-filled abusers, kissing betrayers, the wicked of the earth
do not have the final word, though they escape present justice –
The Son of David the psalmist is Judge of righteousness,

sing the pages of the Holy Book and its eye witnesses;
come like Thomas to the punctured hands and side
of the Resurrected Man, and find, by faith, everlasting proof –

The Lord is the strength of my life;

4.

and hope of my own resurrection,
when my pilgrimage through these populated green hills,
small towns and their gossiping sidewalks,

my sea-side glimpses of the sacramental
in languid, broad-winged gulls,
flying fish cascading over waves,

my marvel at perfect irises, croton leaves,
my swaying to vyélon and chak-chak – when that voyage is done,
the last trumpet calls, and His resurrection has rearranged all,

Of whom shall I be afraid?

XIII

The LORD looks from heaven;
He sees all the sons of men.
From the place of His dwelling He looks
On all the inhabitants of the earth; – Psalm 33:13, 14

1.
In this contentious, contested post-truth world,
Pilate still asks, "What is truth?"
And the street argues, "Whose truth is truth?"

Politicians no longer accept election losses,
denying clear facts of ballot boxes,
absolutes of evidence become convenient

relativities to suit agendas of power
or frenzies of passing opinion,
or to sustain religious theocracies of oppression –

The LORD looks from heaven;

2.
sees the mathematics of logic that shape truth,
and for the dimensions of Spirit revelation
of His sacred creation and cosmic mystery,

He gives faith. Which won't satisfy those
who only believe what they can see and touch
in a material world without soul, without more than

dust, rust, decrepitude, death as irrefutable end,
relieved by pleasures of capital, pyrrhic victories over enemies,
ignoring in their brief lives, from moment to moment, that

He sees all the sons of men.

3.
But many still go in caravans to the Holy City
for the Feast of Weeks, Pentecost, when, yes,
the Holy Spirit of Truth descended

in hurucan wind and urgent tongues of fire,
a Helper to those who believe and receive
the disclosure of God, living Logos,

transcendent and immanent, speaking
the reality of things in nation languages,
in psalms, in ancient books –

From the place of His dwelling He looks,

4.

sends epiphanies of Truth, Goodness, Beauty,
signals of the sacred, from His Sanctuary,
which we receive through the imagination

and the reason of faith with its premises –
and the Spirit says to the churches baptized
with His Presence, remember who you are,

watch yourself under the gaze of Spiritus Mundi,
do not exchange divine truth for fables,
let My Holy Spirit pour abundantly through your faith,

On all the inhabitants of the earth;

XIV

The eyes of the LORD are on the righteous,
And His ears are open to their cry.
The face of the LORD is against those who do evil,
To cut off the remembrance of them from the earth. – Psalm 34:15, 16.

1.
The Apocalypse of John may be phantasmagoric,
with multi-headed scarlet beasts, cataclysmic trumpets and bowls,
but it's not dystopian, not hopelessly grim,

in the symbolic dramas of world history,
prophetic visions of the tomorrow
on whose threshold we stand –

sci-fi movies and chronicles of the fantastic
owe much to this original cosmic tale
of wars in heaven and demons on earth running riot –

The eyes of the LORD are on the righteous,

2.
their names are written in His book of life;
the scroll with seven seals unfolds the world's destiny;
horsemen of famine, war and plagues

already roam cities, islands and continents,
Babylon is falling apart on its democracies and autocracies,
the two witnesses of truth and goodness are assassinated everywhere,

the Dragon sends monsters from sea and earth,
(read state oppression and state-compliant religion),
the redeemed reject the mark of the beast for the Ancient of days,

And His ears are open to their cry.

3.
Even when Gog and Magog surround the Holy City
with nuclear dirty bombs, social media propaganda,
racisms, suppression of rights, blasphemies against the Most High,

and the Little Horn desecrates sacred spaces of creation,
the Alpha and Omega, the elders and creatures around the throne
(read God, His people and the faithful host of the heavenly,)

chant new psalms of victory over the Serpent and his image.
John's prophetic book is rooted in our history,
the visions of its testimony graphically reveal,

The face of the LORD is against those who do evil,

4.

He is always in control, One like the Son of Man,
always with His people, the First and the Last,
alive forevermore, Lord of history.

No Marvel-movie gobbledy-gook here –
from Daniel, Ezekiel and John, ancient prophets,
comes this substance of centuries of faith

that has bound martyrs to burning stakes in Nero's stadia,
to crosses in Sudan, to mockers' scoffings in modern cities –
in this final prophecy, the Root of David has promised the Satanic
hordes

To cut off the remembrance of them from the earth.

XV

Let the LORD be magnified,
Who has pleasure in the prosperity of His servant.
And my tongue shall speak of Your righteousness
And of Your praise all the day long. – Psalm 35: 27, 28

1.
You must now enter the silence alone and listen. Wait.
Wait for the translation of the first line. Write.
Write with your fingers searching pigments on the palate

for the essential shading of the right
image. The medium frames the sacred intercession.
To give face, posture and voice to the holy is no trite

matter. And where humility unveils some gracious incarnation,
offer first this blessed sacrament to the King of saints.
So we sing the holy hymn,

Let the LORD be magnified.

2.
On this scarred island palimpsest, the Master has etched His colophon.
It's the final engraving – after Sumerian clay and Nile papyri,
Macedonian vellum and Lindisfarne

illuminations; after Dead Sea parchments, German incunabula,
and all those versions of His oracles;
in short, the transcripted history of The Book. We

must learn again the alphabet of Eden and Gethsemane's canticles,
and hope to read our names in His unfolding scroll.
We practice the Lectio Divina in His Presence,

Who has pleasure in the prosperity of His servant.

3.
When I remember the angst-ridden sonnets and mincing couplets,
those self-regarding bit parts in pretentious existential dramas,
coffee-and-cigarette nights of self-righteous zealotry –

it's not regret or shame that idly scrolls names
of gone lovers and drifted days. I had lost faith in that circus,
before I found myself in this office copying hours of psalms

(what more can paltry poetry say?) and signing pure colours of
sacred faces
across the illuminating columns of these holy books.
So now I memorise holy writ,

And my tongue shall speak of Your righteousness.

4.

It is not true that Spirit is invisible. He proclaims Himself in
several guises:
astute aphorism, careless cliché, oracular jargon,
declamatory rhetoric, many-costumed metaphor, multiple voices.

Look for the ring of truth, the thumbprint of conviction,
the image of reflection, the turning line.
There is a Voice that speaks beyond incomprehension.

Read faces carefully for the plain
speech of an Artisan who builds tables and universes,
Who is filled with Your awe-full wonder,

And of Your praise all the day long.

XVI

Why are you cast down, O my soul?
And why are you disquieted within me?
Hope in God. For I shall yet praise Him
For the help of His countenance. – Psalm 42:5

1.
October is getting cooler under the breadfruit trees,
with moist air of overcast skies
making mist in hillside gardens,

covering the roads under street lamps
you can see from behind curtains,
roads without footsteps or voices even early

in the night. TV news is the usual menu
of shootings, political sniping, citizens complaining
of something or other – you ask the empty cereal bowl

Why are you cast down, O my soul?

2.
search for any messages on the phone,
get a pyjama shirt for warmth, make some tea
and change the channel from local to BBC

to hear what civilization is plotting now –
with a hard scattering of passing rain
the neighbour starts to play Lucky Dube and Marley loud,

you suck your teeth, turn up the TV sound,
check your messages again, but the world outside
is about its business, which you ought to realise,

And why are you disquieted within me?

3.
The insight comes past tea, Marley and BBC,
many are alone, but not lonely,
and guess what, many are lonely

who are not alone, companions of polite inattention,
social media distractions and their temptations
to emotional infidelities, affections once warm,

now sodden and discarded like that tea-bag.
You reach for faith and its reason,
and some lyric of Marley makes you hum,

Hope in God. For I shall yet praise Him,

4.

alone, but not lonely,
discouraged, dispirited, depressed
(perhaps with the heavy weather);

prayer hovers in the room
with the flickering TV,
rain dripping uncertainly in the distance

on roofs, even as you nod off
over the phone, still waiting for a signalling
image, still muttering habitual thanks

For the help of His countenance.

XVII

Whom have I in heaven but You?
And there is none upon earth that I desire besides You.
My flesh and my heart fail;
But God is the strength of my heart and my portion forever. – Psalm 73: 25, 26.

1.
It's not that death is not a familiar,
strange, intangible, invisible presence
that hovers over small coffins of baby brothers,

carries a strange scent in grandmothers' beds,
is a rumour on Darling Road with news of a shooting,
in your teens, of a neighbour,

and as years tumble quickly over Christmas calendars,
that now relentless ghost turns up
in fatal car-crashes, drownings, loud grave-side wailings of,

Whom have I in heaven but You?

2.
in grief bereft of hope confronted by the empty place,
faith a bottomless hole, and heaven a word
that offers meaningless comfort

to the hollow, vacant space between arms,
echoing with the drumming lament of the chantwel,
"*Misery. Misery.* È*s Daddy mwen ja mò?"*,

is he who forgave my utter folly gone from sight
into all-embracing earth? Is she who took me
into her breasts' deepest enfolding now forever out of reach?

And there is none upon earth that I desire besides You,

3.
you should say to God Who is your life,
but even He commands we cling to the flesh and bone
of the beloved in sanctuaries

of the living, not oblivious of death,
but loving each other in His Presence
while life in our blood is full,

for soon enough, naïve youth will meet the character
of folk-tales and myths, the scythe carrier,
two-faced Basil, the cloaked and hooded skull –

My flesh and my heart fail;

4.
fear of death debilitates,
hard to see around that bend,
beyond that hole in the ground;

but there is good news of an empty hole in an ancient city
from which a brutalized, killed Man walked out,
and His friends have left eye-witness reports

of eating and drinking with Him after He rose,
and that is no *nancitori*, no rumour or fake news;
there is an end appointed, though we still gather now at graves –

But God is the strength of my heart and my portion forever.

XVIII

Turn away my eyes from looking at worthless things,
And revive me in Your way.
Establish Your word to your servant,
Who is devoted to fearing You. – Psalm 119:37,38.

1.
I like Japanese wood-block prints,
the minimalist architecture of fine lines,
very selective palette of dyes that frame

Kabuki characters, tea-house courtesans,
landscapes of Hokusai and Hiroshige,
their apprehension of the floating world which brings

into that light the sad transitory realm of our living
under cherry blossoms and wisteria
in hanging gardens of Kyoto pagodas –

Turn away my eyes from looking at worthless things,

2.
they seem to say from the ubiquitous piton
of Mount Fuji, even as they also sketch
escapist pleasures of the erotic;

we are flesh and spirit in a sacred cosmic space,
we should abhor desecration of our bodies' temples,
hate that sanctuaries of islands, cities, continents decay

with defilements of capital, greed and irreverence.
Our place in the chain of being, holy crafting of word and art,
should lead us to groan always, teach me to pray,

And revive me in Your way.

3.
The tensions of all art are rooted, are they not,
in man's war with himself, with others,
with nature, with God,

however he conceives Deity? – Philip Sherrard
says there is no wholeness/holiness
without God; aesthetics without metaphysics

is a black hole without bottom,
is the beauty of Sodom (says Sherrard). No lecture meant,
but writing the ikon, creating that holy print, is a covenant plea,

Establish Your word to your servant,

4.

bring forth poetry from the poem,
dance from the choreography,
ekphrastic light from the art,

souls' blood song from the music,
let truth, goodness, beauty
be the holy trinity of sacramental epiphany,

by which alone we can challenge
degradation and self-alienation
that everywhere menace aged and youth,

Who is devoted to fearing You.

XIX

Let my soul live, and it shall praise You;
And let Your judgements help me.
I have gone astray like a lost sheep;
Seek Your servant, for I do not forget Your commandments.
– Psalm 119: 175, 176

1.
I often wonder whether the prodigal son
ever went back to the far city
of his dissolute years,

and perhaps, freed from current responsibilities,
searched old companions out,
found former girl-friends who

still remember his close dancing,
smoke-filled rooms, long nights' talk
and all else that followed, before the destitute cry,

Let my soul live, and it shall praise You;

2.
did he locate actors and poets
with whom he knew never-replicated friendships,
centre-stage fame, first books,

quarrels over long-forgotten, long-discarded convictions,
intoxicated travels to islands in their archipelago,
partings at airports, sworn pledges of eternal friendship,

shared funerals of those whose cars crashed;
and, like malevolent ghosts, come again memories of poverty
and abandonment, and the saving husks of his father's psalms,

And let Your judgements help me.

3.

Did he, on that imagined return visit, in fervid remembrances
of past loves, forget himself,
wake in familiar beds,

smoke from stained chalices,
fall once more into old heresies,
applaud futile, still cycling, political hopes,

until, walking by the now upscale neighborhood
of the old swine pen,
remembered himself, and soberly muttered,

I have gone astray like a lost sheep;

4.

I often practice Lectio Divina along those lines.
It's not far-fetched, since all returned prodigals
live flesh and blood reality,

suffer their hearts' turbulences,
emotional roller-coasters, overwhelming desires
of their humanity, tempted by allurements

of Babylon town, disappointed with their own failures,
betrayed by occupational hazards of love –
with the psalmist, these returned prodigals make constant
supplication,

Seek Your servant, for I do not forget Your commandments.

XX – EPILOGUE

I will lift up my eyes to the hills –
From whence comes my help?
My help comes from the LORD,
Who made heaven and earth. – *Psalm 121:1,2*

1.
After poems, psalms. And canticles of island pilgrims
passing through self-important harbours, smoke-blue banana valleys,
villages lounging at curves of bougainvillea lanes. Faith limns

your life salted by Atlantic trades, fretting with Kwéyòl vyélons,
children gone to hard-rock malls of Kingston and Flatbush.
O – in beloved corner shrines of mango blossom, breadfruit palm,
almonds' broad oval

leaf, chapels of sidewalks' hasty awnings, confessionals of indignant
minivans, the fuming censer of streets' sulphur speech –
O, at every wary block – His Real Presence, and archangels gossiping
of His Parousia.
After poems, psalms. And your canticles.

I will lift up my eyes to the hills –

2.
of my island, to Morne Gimie the highest peak,
to twin volcanic cones of Pitons,
to house roofs scattered across green mornes,

under cloud-edged light that lines pastel hues
of multifarious vegetation and sacramental signals
of these numinous landscapes –

a song of ascents rises from somewhere,
an old kwéyòl melody on a vyélon,
perhaps composed by an enslaved woman, lamenting,

From whence comes my help?

3.

All that has gone before in these glosas
were not meant to be a jeremiad,
but the old psalmists always spoke and sung

with prophetic edge into their world,
proclaiming the Mysterium Tremendum of God
in this sacred cosmos,

wrote out against Egypt, Babylon, Rome,
false prophets; made sacrificial offering
for the peoples' sins and their own, crying in ashes,

My help comes from the LORD,

4.

Who sees oppressors, racists, rulers of lies
and deceptions, religion and state collaborators,
corrupt judges, criminals who prey on their own,

abusers of all kinds, those who consort with demons,
who buy and sell the earth and forests, perpetuating poverty,
who traffic in souls and bodies of children, women and men –

Who sees those that extend love, kindness, graciousness
into neighborhoods, use their gifts always
to honour the living LORD

Who made heaven and earth.

AUTHOR'S NOTE:

These poems use the glosa form, "an early Renaissance form that was developed by Spanish poets in the 14th and 15th centuries. The opening quatrain is followed by four stanzas, each of which is generally ten lines long. Each ending line (tenth line) of the four following stanzas is taken from the quatrain. The usual rhyme scheme of a glosa is a final word rhyming of the 6th, 9th and 10th lines."

The quatrains in this cycle of poems come exclusively from the Psalms.

The poems, in the spirit of the psalmist, speak to and out of this Christian poet's personal and collective experience as a world citizen, resident in the Caribbean island of Saint Lucia.

ABOUT THE AUTHOR

JOHN ROBERT LEE (b. 1948) is a St. Lucian writer who has published eleven collections of poetry. His short stories, poems, essays and reviews can be found in many journals (print and online), newspapers and international anthologies. He is the author of *Saint Lucian Writers and Writing: an author Index of published works of poetry, prose and drama* (Papillote Press, 2019).

He has been a teacher, librarian, radio and TV broadcaster, literary journalist, reviewer, editor, newspaper columnist, actor and director. He presently manages an email listserve to Caribbean writers at home and abroad. He is committed to Caribbean Community. He regularly reviews Caribbean Literature for various journals and newspapers. He is a practising Christian, and a preaching elder with a Reformed Baptist Church in Saint Lucia.

Nobel laureate Derek Walcott said of his younger contemporary, "Robert Lee has been a scrupulous poet; that's the biggest virtue he has, and it's not a common virtue in poets, to be scrupulous and modest in the best sense, not to over-extend the range of the truth of his emotions, not to go for the grandiose. He is a Christian poet obviously. You don't get in the poetry anything that is, in sense, preachy or self-advertising in terms of its morality. He is a fine poet."

PRAISE FOR *AFTER POEMS, PSALMS*

John Robert Lee is a singular voice in Caribbean Literature. He is a poet of rare authority, deep insight and profound compassion who walks the shifting boundary line between praise and lament to produce stunning works that intercede for and bide-up humanity. In the way that we might look to the psalms for strength and solace, *After Poems, Psalms* should be received as a gift, a balm and a cause for celebration. Here is a companion to assist spirit wrestlers and lovers of poetry in their quest to identify the numinous in both the human and the natural worlds. Thank you, Robert!

— *Lorna Goodison, Former Poet Laureate of Jamaica, 2017-2020. Her* Collected Poems, Mother Muse, *and* Dante's Inferno: A New Translation *are published by Carcanet Press. She was awarded the Queen's Gold Medal for Poetry in 2019.*

What sustains you is a faith, which feeds your vision. While I do not share your faith, though its languages were fed to me from early, and the poetry I have kept, I do experience your visions, made of nature, inspired by biblical language, by the languages that have been inspired by other poets, their music and words, which have been created to transform the imperial visions which have brought about such obscenities in our world that we have had to save and sustain ourselves, nourish ourselves anew. Of course, there were poets from within those imperial cultures, many, who too sought to remake their world whose abuse of power wreaked havoc. Your work contributes to that remaking. I sense that coming across the water from Guadeloupe and Martinique, Césaire and St John Perse have infected your *glosas*, coming to meet up with Walcott – those immediate ones, but many others, as I say, who you call upon, who have helped you form your own language.

Poems, canticles, psalms – now glosas!

I read your work this way. You call upon beauty, with thanksgiving.

— *Lawrence Scott, Trinidadian novelist and poet. His* Looking for Cazabon, *is published by Papillote Press*

It is always difficult to bring God into poems, lest the words are too slick with resolution, make the poem's journey slide off the page too quickly. Lee's poetry makes us walk shoulder to shoulder with him by the telling way he has arranged the poems – so we traverse through human-voiced verses up to the altar of Scripture. Lee's poems in *After Poems, Psalms* never stop being human as he fleshes out the word into his own pilgrimage of faith. Each time a different journey with a step-by-step struggle. Sometimes historical, sometimes cultural, sometimes as personal as old age. This traversing is done with a quietude of language that is Lee's hallmark. Indeed, E.E. Cummings' words resonate with his style: 'I am a little church, no great cathedral.' Thus, Lee's lamenting lines linger with the transformative power of a steady, searchful prayer.

— *Nancy Anne Miller, Bermudian poet. Her* Selected Poems *is published by Valley Press U.K. 2024.*

Lee's time-assured conviction, his hard-earned resonances, evoke profound rejoicing in landscape, woodsmoke, seasons dry and fecund. His celebrations of Saint Lucian life and memory, of Caribbean society past and present, remain undiminished even in the sharing of his many weighty disquiets. Secure in his faithful observation, Lee conjures privacies and confidences from empty rooms and abandoned street corners, managing to avoid the foreboding despair to which so many poets are gravely susceptible.

There is no hiding behind missals, no sense of a pulpit persona speaking down at you. His is a graceful, silvering intelligence, weaving image, message, textural quality without seeming predictable, complacent or trite. Reminiscent, insightful, often defiant, this voice of Lee speaks its uncomfortable veracity as confidently as it sings its psalms of praise. The work ascends and takes you with it. Full of light… whether panoramic or intimate, Lee delivers his towering truth.

— *Adrian Augier is a Caribbean Laureate of Arts & Letters, recipient of the St Lucia Medal of Merit and an Honorary Doctorate from the University of the West Indies. He is a writer, producer and mas'man. His* Navel String *(poems) was published in 2012.*